MW01440040

Copyright © 2024 Sophron Studies
All rights reserved.

The Holy Bible, English Standard Version® (ESV®)
Copyright © 2001 by Crossway,
a publishing ministry of Good News Publishers.
All rights reserved.
ESV Text Edition: 2016

Unless otherwise indicated, Scripture quotations are from the ESV® Bible (The Holy Bible, English Standard Version®), copyright © 2001 by Crossway, a publishing ministry of Good News Publishers. Used by permission. All rights reserved.

Also Available from Sophron Studies

Women of Faith: a 31-Day Devotional

31 Prayers for Your Baby

31 Prayers for Your Children

31 Prayers for Your Daughter-in-Law

31 Prayers for Your Friend

31 Prayers for Your Grandchild

31 Prayers for Your Son

31 Days: Scripture-Based Prayers for Your Husband

Anchored in Prayer: A Mom's A-Z Prayer Guide Seeking God's Attributes for Their Students

November: The Thankful Challenge

With My Whole Heart: Study Devotionals and Prayers in Psalm 119

Preparing to Celebrate the Savior: An Advent Devotional Study

Revealed: An Inductive Study on Psalm 19

Rest for Weary Souls: An Inductive Study on Psalm 23

Samson: a Glimpse of God's Grace & Mercy: An Inductive Study in Judges 13-16

Ordinary Excellence: An Inductive Study of Proverbs 31

Women Who Worship: An Inductive Study of 8 Women in the Bible

Teach Us to Pray: An Inductive Study on The Lord's Prayer

Redeeming Grace and the Cross of Christ: An Inductive Study in Galatians

Blessed in the Beloved: An Inductive Study in Ephesians

Joy in the Partnership of the Gospel: An Inductive Study in Philippians

Perfect and Complete: An Inductive Study in Colossians

The Gospel of God: An Inductive Study in 1 Thessalonians

Stewarding the Faith: An Inductive Study in 1 Timothy

Remember Jesus Christ: An Inductive Study in 2 Timothy

For the Sake of the Faith: An Inductive Study in Titus

By Faith: An Inductive Study in Hebrews 11

Stable and Steadfast: An Inductive Study in James

Hope Fully: An Inductive Study of 1 Peter

Stability: An Inductive Study in 2 Peter

Kept: An Inductive Study in Jude

*Some studies offer a separate Leader Guide

Trust & Obedience

Do you want to trust God more, even in times of uncertainty, especially when it is extraordinarily challenging? Do you want to have a better prayer life? The Lord's prophet, Elijah, has much to teach! Learn from the man who modeled faithfulness, prayer, and boldness in the face of uncertainty and adversity. May you be enamored with God as you endeavor to understand the life and faith of Elijah. Elijah was a man with a nature like ours--- *you* will be able to relate to the ups and downs of his life.

Each lesson of this inductive Bible study instructs the learner to consider Elijah's life of trust and obedience. Elijah's faith was intriguing and imperfect, counter-cultural, and yet relevant to our faith; he had a nature like yours. Throughout this six-week study, you will be confronted with faith, fear, disappointment, doubts, victory, compassion, and the absolute awe of the living God. Be encouraged to persevere with trust and obedience through your own trials and challenges in your personal faith. Grab a friend or a couple of neighbors and commit to persevere through this short but intense study.

Contents

11	Sophron Studies
13	Guide to Word Definitions
15	Lesson One: Survey
33	Lesson Two: Ravens and Reverence
47	Lesson Three: Fear the Lord
63	Lesson Four: Listening to a Whisper
77	Lesson Five: The Word of the Lord
95	Lesson Six: Elijah's Ministry in Review

Sophron Studies

Sound Doctrine | Sound Thinking | Sound Living

Sophron Studies is a reformed, inductive, in-depth approach to the study of God's word. *Sophron*, pronounced "so-fron," is the Greek word for a sound mind. It is curbing one's desires and impulses with self-control and temperance. As believers, we need to be women who study and delight in God and His word, women who train to have a mind centered on God and renewed by truth (Romans 12:1–2).

A *sophron* mind is God's design for every believer. A *sophron* woman has a wise and sound mind and uses sound judgment; she cultivates prudence and exercises restraint over all her thoughts, whims, plans, passions, and pursuits of desire. A *sophron* woman trains to conform her mind to Jesus Christ: she is single-minded with a governed mind.

A woman who is not *sophron* could struggle with impure and irrational thoughts; she may allow her mind to wander without caution. The mindless woman becomes a forgetful hearer (James 1:25), is sluggish in her walk (Hebrews 6:12), and moves away from the hope of the gospel of our Lord Jesus Christ (Colossians 1:23).

Who is the *sophron* woman? Who is the woman who is not? It may be the same woman! If we are not training our thinking to be captivated with our Savior, we end up divided in our thinking, unstable and fearful. The sober-minded woman can become unrestrained in her mind when she is angered or fearful. The *sophron* woman and the *unsophron* woman could indeed be the same woman.

Sophron Studies is designed to encourage you to stay focused on our only hope, Jesus Christ! Make it a habit to set your mind on the things above (Colossians 3:1–2). Study diligently to know Him through His word, to be a woman of a sound, *sophron* mind.

Sound Doctrine | Sound Thinking | Sound Living

Guide to Word Definitions

**There will be a few word studies in this study.
Please read the following if you need to learn how to look up words to get the Hebrew or Greek definitions.*

When we read Scripture, the Holy Spirit enlightens and teaches God's truth through His word; He enables us to understand His written word. Scripture was not initially written in English, so looking at the author's original Greek or Hebrew words is often helpful. Most every word in the Bible is assigned a number that coordinates with the original language of the Bible: Hebrew for the Old Testament and Greek for New Testament words --- we refer to these numbers as *Strong's* numbers (named after James Strong, creator of the *Strong's Exhaustive Concordance of the Bible*).

The internet has made finding Strong's number and its definition simple. Multiple free resources, such as www.blueletterbible.org or www.biblehub.com, are available.

Studying the original meaning of a word gives insight and elaborates on what our English language has condensed. In this study, the Greek or Hebrew words you are asked to define are provided for you, and the specific words are *italicized,* followed by the *Strong's* number. Enter the provided Strong's number into your internet search engine. You will often be given several websites to consider. Click on your preferred source and read the definitions.

Example of a Greek word study: *distracted 4049.*

Type into your web browser: Strong's Greek *distracted 4049.* You will find the Greek transliteration (a word changed from its original alphabet into the English alphabet), the part of speech, the pronunciation of the Greek word, and the definition. You should find *perispaó* – meaning to draw away, figuratively to be drawn around in the mind, preoccupied.

Practicing this discipline as a part of Bible study will be rewarding!

Lesson One

Survey

To understand Elijah's life and character, we must survey the world leading up to his debut and well-known prayer. This week's homework helps to set the stage and contextualize Elijah's historical background. The guided questions will enable you to understand the scene and scenarios and to know our covenant-keeping God more intimately.

When reading 1 Kings 11-17, consider these markings to help you read with purpose:

- draw a red triangle over the words *Lord/God*
- draw a black circle over the word *sin*
- color all geographical locations green

Part One: The Setting
Read 1 Kings 11

1. What do you learn about God from this chapter? Describe His character. What is He like? What does He do?

2. Consider the facts about God and think about what He is *not* like. What did He *not* do?

3. What are the obvious facts about Solomon from this chapter? Note the phrases *turned away* and *wholly follow*.

4. What had God made clear for His covenant people (I Kings 11:2)? Cross-reference the following:

   Exodus 34:11-16

   Deuteronomy 7:1-6

5. What made King David, Solomon's father, unlike any other king?

> Nevertheless, for David's sake the Lord his God gave him a lamp in Jerusalem, setting up his son after him, and establishing Jerusalem, because David did what was right in the eyes of the Lord and did not turn aside from anything that he commanded him all the days of his life, except in the matter of Uriah the Hittite.
> 1 Kings 15:4-5

6. What resulted from Solomon's *practices* as he grew older (1 Kings 11:9-11)?

> The words of King Lemuel.
> An oracle his mother taught him:
> What are you doing, my son?
> What are you doing, son of my womb?
> What are you doing, son of my vows?
> Do not give your strength to women, your ways to those who destroy kings.
>
> Proverbs 31:1-3

7. What do you think about Solomon's spiritual journey as he aged? How is this a sober reality to practice 2 Peter 1:5-9 (printed below) and persevere in the faith no matter how old you are?

For this very reason, make every effort to supplement your faith with virtue, and virtue with knowledge, and knowledge with self-control, and self-control with steadfastness, and steadfastness with godliness, and godliness with brotherly affection, and brotherly affection with love. For if these qualities are yours and are increasing, they keep you from being ineffective or unfruitful in the knowledge of our Lord Jesus Christ. For whoever lacks these qualities is so nearsighted that he is blind, having forgotten that he was cleansed from his former sins.

8. Think about what you practice and are committed to. How can the frequent things you do contribute to what defines you? Ask the Lord to make you aware of your practices and see if there is anything you frequently do and practice that dishonors him.

9. Cross-reference 2 Samuel 7:9-16 and Psalm 89:36-37. How do you see the grace of God in 1 Kings 11?

10. Add the pertinent historical facts about Solomon to the chart at the end of this lesson.

Part Two: Many Evil Kings
Read 1 Kings 12-16

1. Complete the chart at the end of this lesson to track the various kings.

2. Remember that Israel has only previously had two kings: Saul and David. There was only one kingdom until Solomon's disregard for God. Imagine if Solomon had practiced obedience to God! How could he have known the ongoing consequences of *turning away* from God? What thoughts come to mind?

3. God was not absent, unaware, or silent during the kings' reigns. Note the phrase, *the word of the Lord*, with a yellow highlighter in 1 Kings 12:15, 22-24, 13:1-9, 17-21, 26, 32, 14:18, 15:29, and 16:1, 7, 12, 34.

   *You will refer back to this in the next lesson, too.

4. What did you learn about the *word of the Lord* from the passages you highlighted?

5. What do you learn about God and His sovereignty from 1 Kings 11-16?

6. *The king's heart is a stream of water in the hand of the Lord; he turns it wherever he will (Proverbs 21:1).* How does God's sovereignty affect you?

7. Read 1 Samuel 2:2-10 and note the specific ways you understand the Lord's sovereignty.

8. Meditate on the Lord for His sovereignty, awareness, and capabilities. What are the other attributes of God that you are worshiping today?

Part Three: Religious Practices
Read 1 Kings 12-16

1. What were the religious practices during the reign of the kings before Elijah? See 1 Kings 11:5-8, 12:28-33, 13:33, 14:23-24, 15:12-14, and 16:32-33.

2. What/who was Asherah? Research the practice of Asherah.

3. What do you learn about Baal worship from Numbers 25:1-3 and Judges 2:10-16, 3:1-9?

4. Define the Hebrew word for *Baal 1168*.

5. Research the practice of Baal worship in a Study Bible to add to your learning.

6. What are idolatrous practices today?

7. Why does idol worship provoke God to jealousy? Read the passage to answer:

   And God spoke all these words, saying,

   "I am the Lord your God, who brought you out of the land of Egypt, out of the house of slavery.

   "You shall have no other gods before me.

   "You shall not make for yourself a carved image, or any likeness of anything that is in heaven above, or that is in the earth beneath, or that is in the water under the earth. You shall not bow down to them or serve them, for I the Lord your God am a jealous God, visiting the iniquity of the fathers on the children to the third and the fourth generation of those who hate me..."

   Exodus 20:1-5

8. Is your heart wholly true to the Lord? Are you satisfied with God? Do you feel protected from idolatry because there is no Baal altar nearby? Consider the wicked kings' affections and King David's love and devotion to God (1 Kings 8:61). Pray that your heart would be wholly true to the Lord our God, walking in His statutes and keeping his commandments.

Part Four: King Ahab and His Wife
Read 1 Kings 16:21-34

1. How is King Ahab described?

2. How did Ahab view God (16:28-34)?

3. How did Ahab view his sin (16:31, 33)?

4. Define the Hebrew word *lightly 7043*.

5. Meditate on the thought of taking sin *lightly*. Journal your response:

6. What do you learn about Ahab's wife (1 Ki. 16:21-34)?

7. What is significant about Ahab's marriage to Jezebel? Cross-reference Deuteronomy 7:3-5.

8. How religious were the newlyweds?

9. How did Ahab regard God's word concerning the rebuilding of Jericho (1 Kings 16:34)?

> Joshua laid an oath on them at that time, saying,
>
> "Cursed before the Lord be the man who rises up and rebuilds this city, Jericho.
>
> "At the cost of his firstborn shall he
> lay its foundation,
> and at the cost of his youngest son
> shall he set up its gates."
>
> Joshua 6:26

10. Write out a prayer to God. Confess any ways that you do not highly regard God's word, take sin lightly, or have a rebellious spirit. Ask the Lord to lead you to live a life holy to Him and wholly devoted to Him.

Part Five: Introducing Elijah
Read 1 Kings 17:1 and James 5:17-18

1. List the facts about Elijah from these verses.

2. What did Elijah know to be true of God despite being surrounded by Baal worship in an evil government?

3. How would you characterize Elijah based on the details you have learned about him from these passages?

4. What does Elijah's name mean? Look it up in a Biblical resource or search the Internet.

5. Who was **Judah's** king when Elijah came on the scene in 1 Kings 17?

6. Who was **Israel's** king when Elijah came on the scene in 1 Kings 17?

7. Where did Elijah live during his ministry? Israel or Judah?

8. How is your character and nature like Elijah's (James 5:17-18)?

9. Consider these questions and write a response:

    a) What is our safety against the pervasive spread of evil?

    b) Is God always or sometimes in control of everything, including the weather and the governing officials?

    c) Who is the greatest King? Why can He be trusted?

10. Read from commentary resources to better understand the context that sets the stage for Elijah. What dates are noted by biblical historians, and whom do they credit with authoring 1 Kings?

The Kings
1 Kings 11-16

Use this chart to record historical facts. Fill in this chart while you're studying the foundation for Elijah. What do you want to remember?

King	Highlights
Solomon	
Rehoboam	
Jeroboam	
Nadab	

Abijam/ Abijah	
Asa	
Baasha	
Elah	
Jehoshaphat	
Zimri	

Omri	
Ahab	

Lesson Two

Ravens and Reverence

Part One: By the Brook
Read 1 Kings 17:1-24

1. Write 3-5 bullet points to capture the topics for this chapter.

> **Challenge Work**
>
> How far from home was Elijah when he went to the brook Cherith?

2. What do you think prompted Elijah to pray that Israel would have no rain? Read Deuteronomy 11:13-17.

3. Elijah was a man with a nature like ours, and he prayed fervently that it might not rain, and for three years and six months it did not rain on the earth. Then he prayed again, and heaven gave rain, and the earth bore its fruit (James 5:17-18). Consider these Greek words:

prayed 4336

earnestly/fervently 4335

4. What does it mean that Elijah prayed *fervently*? Research this in a study Bible or commentary and summarize Elijah's prayer practices.

5. Would you, like Elijah, pray for a financial crisis or an economic depression, knowing you would also be affected? What are you *fervently* praying for because of any corrupt leadership and surrounding idolatry?

6. Fervent prayer can be short. Spend a few minutes *praying a prayer*.

7. How did the Lord care for Elijah by the brook Cherith (1 Kings 17)?

8. What do you know about ravens and their hospitality? Use the internet to find a few details about ravens.

9. Did Elijah know how long the Lord would have him stay by the brook Cherith, his food catered by ravens, hiding and alone? How easy is it for us to trust in the Lord when the future is uncertain? Read Psalm 37:1-7.

> Fret not yourself because of evildoers;
> be not envious of wrongdoers!
> For they will soon fade like the grass
> and wither like the green herb.
> Trust in the Lord, and do good;
> dwell in the land and befriend faithfulness.
> Delight yourself in the Lord,
> and he will give you the desires of your heart.
> Commit your way to the Lord;
> trust in him, and he will act.
> He will bring forth your righteousness as the light,
> and your justice as the noonday.
> Be still before the Lord and wait patiently for him;
> fret not yourself over the one who prospers in his way,
> over the man who carries out evil devices!

10. Recall a recent time when the Lord tenderly provided for you before and during a trial. Did you, like Elijah, obey immediately and follow the Lord's leading? Do you practice obedience, or are you known for hesitating, resisting, complaining, or doubting God? Praise God for His love and attentiveness.

Part Two: Elijah and the Nameless Widow
Read 1 Kings 17:1-16 and Luke 4:24-26

1. Organize the details into the chart to help you observe the content.

Text	Command(s)	Location	How God provided	Other details
1 Ki. 17:2-7	*depart* *hide*			
1 Ki. 17:8-16	*arise* *dwell*			

2. What might Elijah have thought of the Lord's purposeful command to go to Zarephath? Note the destination on a map and recall the religion of Sidon (1 Kings 16:31).

3. What do you learn about the widow and her situation?

4. Based on the facts about the widow in #3, describe her and her situation in your own words.

5. Based on the facts about the widow, what was she *not* like?

6. What do you learn from Matthew 10:41-42 (below)?

   The one who receives a prophet because he is a prophet will receive a prophet's reward, and the one who receives a righteous person because he is a righteous person will receive a righteous person's reward. And whoever gives one of these little ones even a cup of cold water because he is a disciple, truly, I say to you, he will by no means lose his reward.

7. Why would the widow, a Baal worshiper, be comforted by God's word (1 Kings 17:14)? How must she have responded to the Lord?

8. How did God prove trustworthy, merciful, and reliable to the widow day by day? How often did the Lord's provisions sustain the widow, her son, and Elijah? How has the Lord prolonged your provisions during trials, isolation, and impending evil? Take time to meditate on your personal history with God, journal your remembrances, and praise God for His continual sustenance, resources, and generosity.

Part Three: Elijah Prayed
Read 1 Kings 17:17-24 and Luke 4:24-26

1. Did the widow have the spiritual maturity to understand and trust God's perfect will? Do you? Does anyone champion through uncertainty and fear? What might the widow have been feeling during her son's illness and death, even though they were saved through the famine?

2. Why did the widow have to suffer more, a trial on top of a trial? How does 1 Peter 1:6-9, 2:21-25, 3:17, 4:12-19, and 5:10 give insight into suffering (1 Kings 17:17-18)?

3. What do you learn about God from 1 Kings 17:17-18, 1 Samuel 2:1-10, and Job 1:21?

4. What did Elijah do for the widow's son (1 Kings 17:17-24)? List the details.

5. Complete the chart below with Elijah's two prayers for the child.

he cried to the Lord (17:20)	*O Lord my God*
he cried to the Lord (17:21)	*O Lord my God*

6. Remember, Elijah had a nature like ours. Evaluate the details of his prayers and write an assessment (e.g., he prayed with emotion, cried out to God, questioned, etc.).

7. He is alive! How does the boy's revival point to Christ? Consider these verses as you answer:

Now after the Sabbath, toward the dawn of the first day of the week, Mary Magdalene and the other Mary went to see the tomb. And behold, there was a great earthquake, for an angel of the Lord descended from heaven and came and rolled back the stone and sat on it. His appearance was like lightning, and his clothing white as snow. And for fear of him the guards trembled and became like dead men. But the angel said to the women, "Do not be afraid, for I know that you seek Jesus who was crucified. He is not here, for he has risen, as he said. Come, see the place where he lay. Then go quickly and tell his disciples that he has risen from the dead, and behold, he is going before you to Galilee; there you will see him. See, I have told you." (Matthew 28:1-7)

...that I may know him and the power of his resurrection, and may share his sufferings, becoming like him in his death...(Philippians 3:10)

Blessed be the God and Father of our Lord Jesus Christ! According to his great mercy, he has caused us to be born again to a living hope through the resurrection of Jesus Christ from the dead... (1 Peter 1:3)

8. How did the widow change her thinking? Creatively write the widow's testimony from 1 Kings 17.

Part Four: A Time for Prayer
Read Matthew 6:9-13

1. Spend time in prayer. Cry out to the Lord for what concerns you and those close to you. Weep, lament, and continue asking the Lord for all you need.

Part Five: the Word of the Lord

Read 1 Kings 17:1-24, 18:1

1. Review the highlighted phrase, the *word of the Lord,* from Lesson One, Part Two.

2. Note your observations about the *word of the Lord* and Elijah, and write a short answer to each prompt below.

   The word of the Lord is...

   The word of the Lord is *not*...

3. Remember King Solomon's practices (1 Kings 11:11). Take a moment to reflect on your personal schedule. Think about your daily spiritual disciplines and your routines. How are you practicing God's word?

4. How does Psalm 119:1-16 reiterate our need for God and His word? Define the Hebrew word for *store up 6845.*

5. I wonder what Elijah did with his time by the brook Cherith. What do you think? How did Elijah learn to *store up* the word of the Lord? What do you do with any downtime to *store up* God's word, to hide truth in your mind and heart? Think about your practices.

>...making the best use of the time, because the days are evil.
>Ephesians 5:16

6. What are the dangers of *not* practicing God's word? Read Hebrews 2:1 and 5:11-14.

7. How did Elijah's commitment to God and His word influence the widow?

8. How does your practice of God's word influence those around you?

9. Is there anything you can do to *long for the pure spiritual milk of the word* (1 Peter 2:2)? How can you crave more Bible? Do you need to alter your spiritual diet? What can you do to fuel your soul with God's word when you cannot have a quiet moment or when your season of life does not lend itself to a routine?

10. Prayerfully reread the Scriptures from today. Write out a prayer asking God to increase your desire for Him.

Lesson Three

Fear the Lord

Part One: Survey
Read 1 Kings 18:1-46

1. What are the main topics in this chapter?

2. Who are the main characters in this chapter?

3. Where does this chapter take place? Locate these places on a map and note the body of water. *Optional: color all geographical locations green.*

4. What do you learn about God from this chapter? Mark *God* and *Lord* with a red triangle.

5. What do you learn about Elijah from this chapter?

6. What is the update on the drought (18:1-2)?

7. What is detailed about Israel's idolatry in this chapter?

8. Meditate on God's character and spend time praising Him.

Part Two: The Troubler of Israel
Read 1 Kings 18:1-19

1. What do you observe about God's commands to Elijah in 1 Kings 17:3 and 18:1?

    Depart from here and turn eastward and hide yourself by the brook Cherith, which is east of the Jordan (17:3).

    Go, show yourself to Ahab, and I will send rain upon the earth (18:1).

2. Describe the setting in Samaria in 18:1-6.

3. List the details about Obadiah.

4. What does it mean to *fear the Lord*? Read these verses to help you answer:

   Let all the earth fear the Lord; let all the inhabitants of the world stand in awe of him! ---Psalm 38:8

   Behold, the eye of the Lord is on those who fear him, on those who hope in his steadfast love, that he may deliver their soul from death and keep them alive in famine. Our soul waits for the Lord; he is our help and our shield. ---Psalm 33:18-20

   The fear of the Lord is the beginning of knowledge; fools despise wisdom and instruction. ---Proverbs 1:7

5. Summarize the conversation between Elijah and Obadiah (18:7-15).

6. How would you characterize Obadiah? Picture him as a real man working, living, and waiting on God.

7. How do you imagine Obadiah breaking the news to Ahab about finding Israel's most wanted man?

8. Describe the confrontation between Ahab and Elijah (18:16-20).

9. Who was the real *troubler of Israel?* Review 1 Kings 16:31-33.

10. Meditate on Elijah's boldness and steadfastness. What is God teaching you through His protection and provisions through uncertain times? Spend time reflecting on God.

Part Three: Two Different Opinions

Read 1 Kings 18:19-40

1. Describe the scene and gathering of people.

2. How did Elijah rebuke the Israelites (18:21)?

3. How serious were the Israelites with their religion? Define *limping 6452*.

4. What are some religious opinions that people dance or limp between today?

5. Cross-reference these passages and note what you learn about worship:

   Exodus 20:1-6

   Leviticus 20:6

   Psalm 97:7

   Matthew 22:36-37

   2 Corinthians 11:3

6. Scripture describes idolatry as turning from God to worship something or someone else. Define the Greek word for *idolatry 1495*.

7. Read the following verses and highlight the facts about idolatry.

But now I am writing to you not to associate with anyone who bears the name of brother if he is guilty of sexual immorality or greed, or is an idolater, reviler, drunkard, or swindler-- not even to eat with such a one.
---1 Corinthians 5:11

Or do you not know that the unrighteous will not inherit the kingdom of God? Do not be deceived: neither the sexually immoral, nor idolaters, nor adulterers, nor men who practice homosexuality. ---1 Corinthians 6:9

Therefore, my beloved, flee from idolatry. I speak as to sensible people; judge for yourselves what I say. The cup of blessing that we bless, is it not a participation in the blood of Christ? The bread that we break, is it not a participation in the body of Christ? Because there is one bread, we who are many are one body, for we all partake of the one bread. Consider the people of Israel: are not those who eat the sacrifices participants in the altar? What do I imply then? That food offered to idols is anything, or that an idol is anything? No, I imply that what pagans sacrifice they offer to demons and not to God. I do not want you to be participants with demons. You cannot drink the cup of the Lord and the cup of demons. You cannot partake of the table of the Lord and the table of demons. ---1 Corinthians 10:14-21

...exchanged the glory of the immortal God for images resembling mortal man and birds and animals and creeping things. --- Romans 1:23

For you may be sure of this, that everyone who is sexually immoral or impure, or who is covetous (that is, an idolater), has no inheritance in the kingdom of Christ and God. ---Ephesians 5:5

Formerly, when you did not know God, you were enslaved to those that by nature are not gods. But now that you have come to know God, or rather to be known by God, how can you turn back again to the weak and worthless elementary principles of the world, whose slaves you want to be once more? --- Galatians 4:8-9

Put to death therefore what is earthly in you: sexual immorality, impurity, passion, evil desire, and covetousness, which is idolatry. --- Colossians 3:5

But as for the cowardly, the faithless, the detestable, as for murderers, the sexually immoral, sorcerers, idolaters, and all liars, their portion will be in the lake that burns with fire and sulfur, which is the second death. --- Revelation 21:8

Outside are the dogs and the sorcerers and the sexually immoral and murderers and idolaters, and everyone who loves and practices falsehood. ---Revelation 22:15

8. Was Baal worship worse than our own idolatry? Explain the sin of idolatry.

9. It is unlikely that you are a Baal worshiper, but is it possible that you have idols and limp between two different opinions? Do you covet what you do not have or doubt God's sufficiency? What interferes with your pure devotion to God? Take time to reflect on your heart with honesty as you contemplate idolatry.

10. Praise God for grace and forgiveness.

> If we confess our sins,
> he is faithful and just
> to forgive us our sins and
> to cleanse us from all unrighteousness.
>
> 1 John 1:9

Part Four: The Contest
Read 1 Kings 18:20-37

1. How did the Baal worshipers prepare their bull?

2. Describe how the people waited for their god to act.

3. How did Baal respond to the people's expectations?

4. How did Elijah prepare for God's glory to be shown?

5. Consider the prayers:

Baal worshipers	Elijah
O Baal, answer us! (18:26) They cried aloud and cut themselves after their custom with swords and lances, until the blood gushed out upon them (18:28). They raved on until the time (18:29).	*O Lord, God of Abraham, Isaac, and Israel, let it be known this day that you are God in Israel, and that I am your servant, and that I have done all these things at your word. Answer me, O Lord, answer me, that this people may know that you, O Lord, are God, and that you have turned their hearts back. (18:36-37).*

6. What can you learn from Elijah's prayer?

7. How did God reveal His power and glory (18:38)? Did they still *differ between two opinions* even after God showed Himself?

8. How did the people respond to God's power and mercy (1 Kings 18:39)?

9. What became of the prophets of Baal?

10. Prayerfully reflect on what convinced you to stop *limping* between two different opinions--- the world and God--- and acknowledge God's power, strength, and mercy.

Part Five: The Lord, He is God
Read 1 Kings 18:20-46

1. What have you learned about God this week? What do you think about His display of power, grace, and mercy?

2. How might Elijah have felt physically, mentally, emotionally, and spiritually after 18:40? Consider Elijah's humanity and journal your response.

3. What did Elijah tell Ahab to do (1 Kings 18:41-42)? What did Ahab do? Why?

4. Describe King Ahab's character.

5. What did Elijah do while Ahab went to eat and drink at the sound of the rushing of rain?

> Elijah was a man with a nature like ours, and he prayed fervently that it might not rain, and for three years and six months it did not rain on the earth. Then he prayed again, and heaven gave rain, and the earth bore its fruit.
>
> James 5:17-18

6. What is your impression of 1 Kings 18:42-44?

7. If you are creative, sketch the scene from 1 Kings 18:45-46. If you are less artistic, record the details of the setting.

8. Why did Elijah run ahead of the chariot, and Ahab rode in his chariot? Consider these possibilities:

   Elijah loved running, and he was fast

   or

   Elijah ran ahead of the king's chariot as a way of showing respect for the king's position in government

   or

   (write your own reason here)

9. Read from commentary resources to gain insight into 1 Kings 18:1-46.

10. Compare your personal prayer routine to Elijah's commitment to prayer. What do you fervently pray about? What motivates you to keep praying the same prayer over and over? Spend time reflecting on the privilege of worship and praise God that He hears, cares, and responds.

Lesson Four

Listening to His Whisper

Part One: Death Threat
Read 1 Kings 19:1-8, 10, 14

1. It rained! Why did Jezebel's heart not soften at the supernatural display of God's power and mercy? Why did she assume Elijah was not a threat to her even though he killed all the prophets of Baal with the sword? What did Jezebel determine to do?

> And this is the judgment: the light has come into the world, and people loved the darkness rather than the light because their works were evil. For everyone who does wicked things hates the light and does not come to the light, lest his words should be exposed.
> John 3:19-20

2. Define *afraid 7200*.

3. Consider 1 Kings 19:3 in the KJV.

> And when he saw that, he arose, and went for his life, and came to Beersheba, which belongeth to Judah, and left his servant there.

4. What had Elijah realized about the people of Israel and their devotion to God (18:39 and 19:10)? What did he lament as he sat under the broom tree? Also, read the apostle Paul's words in Romans 11:1-6 (below).

> I ask, then, has God rejected his people? By no means! For I myself am an Israelite, a descendant of Abraham, a member of the tribe of Benjamin. God has not rejected his people whom he foreknew. Do you not know what the Scripture says of Elijah, how he appeals to God against Israel? "Lord, they have killed your prophets, they have demolished your altars, and I alone am left, and they seek my life." But what is God's reply to him? "I have kept for myself seven thousand men who have not bowed the knee to Baal." So too at the present time there is a remnant, chosen by grace. But if it is by grace, it is no longer on the basis of works; otherwise grace would no longer be grace.

5. Was Jezebel's death threat to Elijah a consideration he should fear? Had Elijah come to Beersheba because he was afraid the Queen would execute him, or was there perhaps a sense of hopelessness and disappointment with those he cared for? Was he in disobedience to God? Explain your answer.

6. When have your loved ones or colleagues seen a supernatural display of God's power and made a profession of faith, only to turn back to the world's comfort? How do you reconcile their faithlessness when God has clearly answered prayer and shown mercy, but they do not persevere in faith?

7. How did God display His grace and mercy to Elijah?

8. How does God offer comfort and sustenance to us when we are troubled, discouraged, frustrated, and overwhelmed? Cross-reference these passages:

   Psalm 23:1-6

   Psalm 34:18

   Psalm 147:3

   2 Corinthians 1:3-9

9. Read from multiple commentary resources on 1 Kings 19:1-8.

10. How has the Lord tenderly cared for you in times of hopelessness and disappointment? Meditate on the times you've been physically, mentally, and spiritually exhausted. How have you experienced the Lord's provisions? Praise God for His fatherly care.

Parts Two & Three: A Thin Silence
Read 1 Kings 19:8-21

1. Note the details of Elijah's travel and lodging.

> **Challenge Work**
>
> What is known of Horeb?

2. Summarize the conversation between Elijah and God.

3. What can you learn from Elijah's pouring out his heart to God?

4. How did God remind Elijah of His might and power (19:11-13)?

5. How did Elijah hear the Lord?
   Check your Bible's footnote for verse twelve.

6. How/when do you hear the Lord? How do you create quiet times and quiet spaces in the middle of loud, chaotic, overly stimulated situations so that you can pay attention to God's word and experience His work in your life?

7. How did Elijah respond to God?

8. How did Elijah *not* respond when God made Himself available? What did he *not* do?

9. What information did God share with Elijah (19:15-18)? Write the instructions and then observe and evaluate the list.

10. How do you think 1 Kings 19:18 encouraged Elijah?

11. Was Elisha expecting the call to ministry? Explain your answer.

12. Is serving in ministry typically convenient? How do you switch gears when you feel the Lord prompting you to serve while in the middle of a project, a career, etc.?

13. Research this unusual call to ministry using a commentary to better understand the plan of *casting the cloak*.

14. How can this humble servant, Elisha, encourage us to serve humbly?

15. What is your response to 1 Kings 19:8-21? There have been a lot of events, feelings, and plans. Consider Elijah as a real person like yourself, meditate on what you have learned, and journal your response.

Part Four: Elijah is Back
Read 1 Kings 21:1-29

1. What are your impressions of this story and its main characters?

    Naboth

    Ahab

    Jezebel

2. How did Elijah approach Ahab when he returned to Samaria?

3. How do you think Elijah may have felt about confronting Ahab again?

4. How did Ahab refer to Elijah (21:20)?

5. What was Ahab's judgment for doing evil in the sight of the Lord (21:21-25)?

6. What is the summary of Ahab's life (21:25-26)?

7. How did Ahab show remorse for his wicked ways?

8. How did God respond to Ahab's remorse?

9. Look deeper into God's mercy and holy expectations for His people. Cross-reference the following verses:

   Micha 6:8

   Colossians 3:12

James 2:13

James 4:6

1 Peter 1:3

10. Of all that Elijah had to endure with wicked Ahab, how do you think he responded to Ahab's humility and God's mercy toward him? What is your response to God's mercy toward violent, vicious, wicked people? Is there an evil ruler deserving of disaster that you can pray for? Praise God for His mercy, patience, and _____. As you struggle to forgive, ask the Lord for His help.

Part Five: Prophecies Fulfilled

Read more of Ahab's and Jezebel's stories in 1 Kings 22 and 2 Kings 9, 10

1. Enjoy today's reading. Take notes as needed to help you remember the facts and keep the details straight. These are just for you, so make the most of this devotional time with God.

2. Who will God always care for? Cross-reference Psalm 37:1-2, 9 and Proverbs 11:21, 12:7.

3. What have you learned about God this week?

4. What is one thing you have learned about yourself this week?

5. Read from commentary resources to help you better understand the many historical events.

6. Praise God for His purposes, plans, sovereignty, and mercy.

Lesson Five

The Word of the Lord

Parts One & Two: Ahaziah's Accident
Read 2 Kings 1:1-18

1. Who is this chapter about? List what you learn about God. Who is He? What is He like? What does He do?

2. What are the themes in this chapter?

3. List the facts about Ahaziah from 1 Kings 22:40-53.

4. What should King Ahaziah have been considering on his deathbed for his people and country (2 Kings 1:1)?

5. Describe the depth of Ahaziah's spiritual blindness and hard heart. Define *Baal-zebub 1176* and cross-reference Matthew 12:24, 27.

6. What is idolatry? *Review Lesson Three (page 53).*

7. See the following passages and note what you learn about idolatry.

Exodus 32:1-5

Job 31:24-28

Jeremiah 10:5

Colossians 3:5-11

1 John 5:21

8. Read Exodus 20:1-7 and explain the seriousness of worshipping the only God.

9. Think about Ahaziah's arrogance and refusal to acknowledge God. Summarize the king's attempts to bring Elijah to himself (2 Kings 1:9-14).

10. Compare the captains:

Captain #1 and #2	Captain #3

11. How do you relate to Ahaziah's curiosity regarding his future? Are you patient while anticipating what's next? How do you practice trusting God while waiting for Him to unfold His plan?

Be still before the Lord and wait patiently for him... (Psalm 37:7a).

For God alone my soul waits in silence; from him comes my salvation. He alone is my rock and my salvation, my fortress; I shall not be greatly shaken (Psalm 62:1-2).

12. How did God show mercy to Ahaziah's life?

13. Read over these verses and meditate on God's mercy.

The Lord is merciful and gracious, slow to anger and abounding in steadfast love (Psalm 103:8).

The steadfast love of the Lord never ceases; his mercies never come to an end; they are new every morning; great is your faithfulness (Lamentations 3:22-23).

"For I will be merciful toward their iniquities, and I will remember their sins no more." Hebrews 8:12

But God being rich in mercy, because of the great love with which he loves us, even when we were dead in our trespasses, made us alive together with Christ---by grace you have been saved--- and raised us up with him and seated us with him in the heavenly places in Christ Jesus... (Ephesians 2:4-5).

...He saved us, not because of works done by us in righteousness, but according to his own mercy, by the washing of regeneration and renewal of the Holy Spirit... (Titus 3:5).

Blessed be the God and Father of our Lord Jesus Christ! According to his own mercy, he has caused us to be born again to a living hope through the resurrection of Jesus Christ from the dead (1 Peter 1:3).

14. Meditate on a recent experience with God's mercy toward you.

15. Is God your first consideration? Are you quick to consult Him in your time of need? Is He your confidante when you struggle? How about when you hear good news, do you praise Him first? Prayerfully consider what tempts you toward idolatry and confess any misplaced worship.

16. Consider these prayers:

    Father, You are worthy of all honor and praise. You are a mighty and powerful God. You are also approachable, compassionate, and loving. You are _____. These verses on idolatry are informative and convicting. It boggles my mind that Aaron would make a golden calf; it seems he was so interested in showcasing something physical that he manifested a small cow, and that sufficed as worthy of worship. That was Aaron, who had seen and experienced your power and might.

As I consider my own heart and the worthless things my mind and hands seek to produce to showcase something worthy, I give too much consideration to _____ and _____. Like scarecrows in a cucumber field, so worthless are my endeavors to find value in money, status, relationships, and _____ (Jer. 10:5).

My soul is weary from _____. I know that only You can satisfy me. Help me to trust You, Your timing, and Your abilities---nothing is beyond Your interference. You can do what seems impossible.

King Ahaziah must have been frantic and frightened about the future. He would not be satisfied in worshiping You and looked elsewhere. Lord, help me to recognize misplaced confidence and trust; show me the worthless idols. Help me to acknowledge sinful desires that entice me to overvalue their misleading worth. Where am I turning for answers instead of seeking You? Help me discern the temptations to sin, quick solutions, and escape routes that are not of You. Sometimes my heart is overcome with anxiety as I sense tension inside my body, and I am fearful of the future, fearful of _____. You know, You are aware, You care. Help me to wait patiently for You. May the peace of Christ rule in my heart. Nothing and no one can satisfy me. Will You comfort my weary soul?

You and only You are worthy of my adoration, time, and attention. You are my worship. Forgive me for anger, wrath, malice, slander, and obscene talk. Forgive me for _____.

Help me to put off the old self with its practices and to put on the new self. God renew my mind in the knowledge of You, my Creator. Forgive me for looking for tangible help when only You can help me. Forgive my idolatry.

Help me to put on a compassionate heart, kindness, humility, meekness, and patience. Please help me to bear with others with a forgiving spirit. You have forgiven me. Father, help me put on love, which binds everything together perfectly.

17. Will you also pray for those who are lost and have misplaced their worship in a false god? Are they beyond God's reach? Are they too deaf to hear God's word? Pray for the men and women who think there is no God in the world worth their time and attention, those who inquire of false gods. Trust the Lord's ability to reach whomever He will choose.

Part Three: Final Moments
Read 2 Kings 2:1-18

1. What is the repeated fact about the Lord in this chapter?

2. Where does this chapter take place? Color all geographical locations green. Trace Elijah's travel on a map.

3. How did God reveal His plan for Elijah's departure?

   ...for the Lord has sent me as far as _____ (2)

   ...for the Lord has sent me to _____ (4)

   ...for the Lord has sent me to the _____ (6)

4. Do you sometimes wish God would give you the overall plan for your life or all the particulars for a season or situation? How does 2:1-6 comfort you as you wait for the Lord's plans to unfold, bit by bit? Cross-references these verses:

Psalm 32:8

Isaiah 30:20-21

Isaiah 58:11

5. What helps you *see* and trust as you wait on the Lord? Meditate on Psalm 119:105.

> Your word is a lamp to my feet
> and a light to my path.

6. Take a moment to pray for the circumstances in your life that you want answers to. Acknowledge God's abilities and sovereignty as you pray; He knows. Remember, you can ask Him for information in your prayers. Here is a prayer to consider to get you started:

Father, You are sovereign over all things. I know You know all the details surrounding my life and these circumstances regarding _____. Help me to trust You. I confess my impatience as I wait. Will You strengthen my mind and body as I wait? Make my bones strong. May I be like a well-watered garden and like a spring of water whose waters do not fail. Overcome my weakness with strength and ability. Will You counsel me with _____ and help me regarding _____?

7. Why do you think Elisha insisted on journeying with Elijah? Recall his role in Elijah's life (1 Kings 19:16, 21).

8. What did the sons of prophets in Bethel and Jericho say to Elisha (2 Kings 2:3-5)? What had God made clear to them?

9. What was Elisha's response to the prophets' prophecy about Elijah?

10. How would you title 2 Kings 2:1-18?

Part Four: Elijah and the Chariot
Read 2 Kings 2:1-18

1. Describe Elijah's final walk as he waited on the Lord.

2. How was crossing the Jordan river made possible?

3. What is significant about Elijah's cloak? Circle the word *cloak* in 2 Kings 2:8,14 and note what you learn about Elijah's cloak. Also, review 1 Kings 19:13-21.

4. Moses and Joshua were also instruments that God used to show His power and authority over water to provide passage (Exodus 14:21 and Joshua 3-4). How did Jesus also display His control over the wind and sea? See Matthew 8:23-27.

5. Cross-reference Proverbs 8:29 and meditate on the One who controls it all.

6. Do you believe that God is in control of the boundaries of water? Can He control the boundaries of your life?

   a) What do you fear may be out of God's control? Take a moment to note these personal fears before God.

   b) How can you self-counsel to set your mind on the almighty and powerful God in charge of the boundaries of the waters and everything else? Meditate on these truths to steady your mind.

7. Summarize the conversation between Elijah and Elisha after they crossed the Jordan.

8. This was a real goodbye. What do you imagine Elijah had on his mind? How different was Elijah's mindset from King Ahaziah's final thoughts? Journal your thoughts.

Part Five: Taken Up
Read 2 Kings 2:1-18

1. What do you imagine when you consider Elijah's final moments? Reflect on the text as you humanize Elijah, a man with a nature like ours.

2. What is a heavenly whirlwind? Define *whirlwind 5591*.

3. How powerful is a whirlwind? Cross-reference a few of these passages: Job 38:1, Psalm 83:15, 107:25; Isaiah 40:24, 41:16; Jeremiah 23:19, 30:23; Ezekiel 13:11, Jonah 1:4, and Zechariah 9:14.

4. Meditate on these verses and sketch the scene that comes to mind with the chariots of fire and horses of fire and the whirlwind taking Elijah up to heaven.

5. How does the text detail Elisha's response to Elijah's departure?

6. Read Genesis 5:24 and how Enoch was also taken. What do these two stories indicate about eternal life?

7. Read more details on 2 Kings 2:1-18 from commentary resources.

8. To conclude this week's lesson, consider how Elijah's ministry affected Israel. What had he done to serve Israel? Praise God for His sovereign plan, for Elijah's ministry, and His perpetual care for His people.

Lesson Six

Elijah's Ministry in Review

Part One: Review
Review 1 Kings 11-16, 17-22, 2 Kings 1-2 and Lessons One-Five

1. What have you learned about God through this study of Elijah? *Take time to flip through your book.*

2. How did God reveal His mercy, grace, and love to the Israelites during Elijah's time? *Give specific examples.*

3. Elijah served the Lord through generations of kings. What was he faithful to do? What have you learned from Elijah's trust and obedience?

4. What was the repeated theme of Elijah's messages to Israel and her kings?

5. King Solomon and many others were not *wholly devoted* to God and turned away from Him. Why did Elijah persist in faith and obedience despite the depravity and worldliness surrounding him?

6. What do you learn about endurance from these verses?

    But the one who endures to the end will be saved (Matthew 24:13).

    Therefore, since we have been justified by faith, we have peace with God through our Lord Jesus Christ. Through him we have also obtained access by faith into this grace in which we stand, and we rejoice in hope of the glory of God. Not only that, but we rejoice in our sufferings, knowing that suffering produces endurance, and endurance produces character, and character produces hope, and hope does not put us to shame, because God's love has been poured into our hearts through the Holy Spirit who has been given to us (Romans 5:1-5).

As for you, always be sober-minded, endure suffering, do the work of an evangelist, fulfill your ministry. (2 Timothy 4:5).

Therefore, since we are surrounded by so great a cloud of witnesses, let us also lay aside every weight, and sin which clings so closely, and let us run with endurance the race that is set before us, looking to Jesus, the founder and perfecter of our faith, who for the joy that was set before him endured the cross, despising the shame, and is seated at the right hand of the throne of God. (Hebrews 12:1-3)

7. Why do you persist in faith and obedience despite the depravity and worldliness surrounding you? Spend time praying that you will rejoice in the hope of God's glory, realizing how His love has been poured into your heart. Also, prayerfully ask the Lord if there are weights and sins that you need to lay aside to prioritize Him, enduring to the end.

Part Two: Prayerfulness

Read James 5:17-18 and review 1 Kings 17-18

1. Why did Elijah pray for no rain (1 Kings 17-18)?

2. Review the definition of *fervent* (see Lesson Two, Part One).

3. How did God answer Elijah's prayer for no rain (1 Kings 17-18)? List the specific evidences in Scripture.

4. How does Romans 12:12 and Ephesians 6:18 encourage you?

5. What do you learn from Elijah about the importance of devoted quiet time with God? Why pray?

6. How have you been convicted about prayer? Are you praying more for your country, government, and even a spiritual revival? How is God answering your prayers?

7. Creatively write a three-point philosophy of prayer from Elijah's perspective (use specific texts from 1 and 2 Kings when Elijah prayed or his communion with God was implied).

   o

   o

   o

8. How did Elijah have a *nature* like ours (James 5:17-18)? Spend time meditating on this and journal your response.

Part Three: Elijah and John the Baptist
Read Luke 1:5-17, 76-80

1. What was the prophecy concerning John the Baptist?

2. How did Luke compare John the Baptist's ministry to Elijah's?

> **Reflections**
>
> How would you describe the *spirit and power* of Elijah?

3. What was prophesied about John the Baptist? Cross-reference Malachi 4:5-6, and then read Matthew 11:13-14.

4. How did John the Baptist identify himself? See John 1:19-27.

5. Compare the two men and their messages:

Elijah	John the Baptist

6. Was John the Baptist Elijah? Explain your answer.

7. Cross-reference Acts 3:12-26. What does this passage tell us about the prophets?

8. What did Peter and John preach in Acts 3:19?

   a) Define *repent 3340*.

   b) Define *turn back 1994*.

9. Review King Solomon's influential demise in 1 Kings 11:1-13 and Elijah's ongoing message to Israel (1 Kings 18:37). Reflect on the Bible's message of repentance and turning back to God.

10. Read from commentary resources to gain more insight concerning John the Baptist's comparison to Elijah (Luke 1:5-17, 76-80).

Part Four: Elijah and the Transfiguration
Read Matthew 17:1-13, Mark 9:2-13, and Luke 9:28-36

1. Summarize the transfiguration.

2. Define *transfigured 3339*.

3. What did Peter, James, and John see and hear from the cloud? Answer in the form of emojis available to you on your smartphone (i.e., sunshine).

4. How did the disciples respond to the transfiguration?

5. What is significant about Moses and Elijah?

   "Do not think that I have come to abolish the Law or the Prophets; I have not come to abolish them but to fulfill them." ---Matthew 5:17

6. What did Jesus declare about Elijah from the Q&A below?

   And as they were coming down the mountain, Jesus commanded them, "Tell no one the vision, until the Son of Man is raised from the dead." And the disciples asked him, "Then why do the scribes say that first Elijah must come?" He answered, "Elijah does come, and he will restore all things. But I tell you that Elijah has already come, and they did not recognize him, but did to him whatever they pleased. So also the Son of Man will certainly suffer at their hands." Then the disciples understood that he was speaking to them of John the Baptist. ---Matthew 17:9-13

7. Scripture helps us understand Scripture. Cross-reference Matthew 14:3, 10-11 to understand Matthew 17:12.

8. Reflect on today's passages that detail the transfiguration. How do you have a better understanding of Elijah?

9. Read from commentary resources concerning the transfiguration.

10. Meditate on Philippians 3:20-21.

> But our citizenship is in heaven, and from it we await a Savior, the Lord Jesus Christ, who will transform our lowly body to be like his glorious body, by the power that enables him even to subject all things to himself.

Part Five: In Conclusion
Continue reviewing Lessons 1-6 and read again 1 Kings 17-22, 2 Kings 1-2

1. Describe Elijah's character in five words.

2. Which of all the stories about Elijah is the most remarkable to you?

3. What would you write or etch on Elijah's tombstone?

4. How does Elijah point to Christ?

5. Consider the great commandments according to Jesus in Matthew 22:36-40. How did Elijah embody love for God and His people?

6. How has Elijah's example influenced your trust and obedience to the Lord? How has his faith encouraged yours? How has the prophet's love for undeserving neighbors spurred you on? Take time to consider how God's word has worked in your life.

7. Praise God for His faithfulness.

We would love to hear from you as you learn to study inductively and as you learn more about our Lord through Elijah's life and faith. Visit our website at www.sophronstudies.com or email us at mysophronstudies@gmail.com.

Do you want to continue studying? Check out the sequel and study Elisha with us!

Sophron Studies